British Haiku S
Members' Anthology 2016

BRITISH HAIKU SOCIETY

FOUNDED 1990

Editor: Shrikaanth Krishnamurthy
Assistant Editor: Pruthvi Shrikaanth (10 years)

Layout & photographs: Shrikaanth Krishnamurthy

Cover Photo &Design: Shrikaanth Krishnamurthy

Inside Art: Shrikaanth Krishnamurthy (Pp 27, 33, 45, 51, 69, 87 & 97)
Sahana Shrikaanth (Pp 9, 21 & 79)

ISBN: 978-1-906333-05-8

Published by:-

The British Haiku Society,
Flat 4,
2 Clifton Lawns,
Ramsgate, Kent
United Kingdom
CT11 9PB

Additional copies of this anthology are available at the cost of £4.00 (including p&p).

Introduction

It was at the AGM last year that I put my hand up to edit this year's anthology. And my son, Pruthvi, faithfully followed suit.

The theme for this year is "Beginning". It was fascinating to see the different takes on the theme, and the variety of form from the various poets. While we had some submissions early on, unsurprisingly, the majority chose to submit in the last couple of weeks prior to the deadline, having us responding to over a hundred poets in the last two weeks or so. Most poets chose to submit more than one offer, which was great as we could choose what we thought would best fit the theme and showcase the haijin's talent.

We were touched by the kind words and sentiment expressed by some of the poets, thanking us for our efforts. And it sure was nostalgic to receive some of the submissions in the post.

We are grateful to all of you that took time to offer your haiku for this selection, and for considering my few editorial suggestions in good spirit. And it sure was fun talking to some of you over the phone. My thanks to Frank Williams for patiently answering all my questions about bringing the anthology together. Again, thanks to him and Dave Serjeant for their help in choosing my haiku.

We have arranged the poems around broad themes which will likely be evident from the art work that precedes each section, and also from the haiku themselves.

Special thanks to my wife Sahana Shrikaanth, for managing to come up with some lovely art work at the last minute, to humour the editor's whim. She also proofread the final draft. Thanks also to the printers for doing a fine job in a short time.

With a record 149 haijin included, this is hitherto the largest annual anthology from the Society. It is with great pleasure we bring this to you. We trust you will enjoy this immensely.

Shrikaanth Krishnamurthy
Pruthvi Shrikaanth

hints of blue
between clouds
the return of spring

- Joanna Ashwell

early spring
a feather blows in
the cat door

- Ernest J. Berry

spring snow
scribbling the bark
a rooster crows

- Marilyn Fleming

cockerel crows at dawn
wild winds drag spring unwilling
to sit by my fire

- Leo McNeir

thawing
d
r
i
p
p
i
n
g
moonbeams

- Shrikaanth Krishnamurthy

the first unfurling
of hazel leaves
sparkling rapids

- Jo Pacsoo

in the teeth of the wind cherry in first bloom

- Jane McBeth

fuchsia tree
its flowers about to burst
into perfume

- Diarmuid Fitzgerald

called to look
irises fielding the first
bumble bee

- Colin Oliver

homeless camp
a jigger of spring rain
in the robin's egg

- Autumn Noelle Hall

grey day:
poppies not quite ready
to burst red

- Maeve O'Sullivan

hard pruned honeysuckle tendrils skyward again

- Lois Lodge

in the washes
fresh green blades of flag
peewits wheeze

- Helen Baker

fresh-cut grass
the rosé promise
of spring

- Keely Khoury

study day
sun-filled
gladioli

- Rose Ades

hilltop garden
an old man
planting beans

- Matt Morden

i pray yours has been
a fortunate rebirth~
first butterfly

- Keith J. Coleman

in the bud
of a crimson rose
a pair of ants

- Patricia Prime

fruit buds
the fledgling's wings
open to the wind

- Klaus-Dieter Wirth

the first day
of the hot season
a broken pot

- Michael Fessler

Chandigarh –
stepping from the train
into the oven

- Sue Lewis

summer solstice
the wood reaches out
to greet me

- David Bingham

pruning time
I apologise
to the bees

- Mary Hind

place your bets
the first raindrops
on the windowpane

- Christopher Radcliffe

towards dawn
the hesitant tap of rain
explains everything

- Susan Lee Kerr

the day's first squall --
hail has the bullocks dash
for hawthorn cover

(nr. Chapelknowe, Dumfries, 9.6.11)

- Tito

top of the mountain
every falling raindrop
assigned a catchment

- David J. Kelly

weather forecast
a pitter-patter
on the tabla

- Hazel Hall

playground emptying a light rain upon the air

- Anthony Marcoff

a later light-
some hesitating
cock-a-doodle

- Marc May

warm up -
the jogger
kicking mist

- Jonathon Iddon

autumn morning
a vapour train sets off
towards the sun

- Margery Newlove

October, the first
light brown touches
on the old oak

- David Ball

weaker sun
ancient beech trees slide
to copper hues

- Paul Hickey

morning mist
mind & eyes follow
a falling leaf

- Frank Williams

falling leaves
the lemonade changes
to cider

- Marilyn Ashbaugh

sun low
a friend plays
a rustling tune

- Chris Southam

sweeping dead leaves
from the neighbour’s path
we start to talk

- Graham Duff

autumn sunrise
the road sweeper's trolleyful
of brushes

- David Jacobs

adding some voice
to its colour --
autumn twilight

- Brendon Kent

early morning dew
mushroom hunting
hands touch

- Sue Richards

maple leaf
in the gutter
collecting rain

- Michael Dylan Welch

the barley has turned –
already the birdsong
is changing its tune

- David Davies

autumn's soft shoe-in another compost pile

- Susan Diridoni

staccato plopping
under the riverside oaks
as they shed acorns

- Alan Maley

day break
watching the light return
just enough for winter

- Liz Jordan

first bite in the air
I wonder where I put my gloves
last April

- Kate B. Hall

buttered toast
the crunch and glide
of this frosty morning

- Gillian Dawson

first flake...
a fall into
winter

- Pat Geyer

dawn
the mountains have turned
very white

- Barbara Anne Morton

wind-loaded snow
the shapes foxed
by morning

- Alan Summers

the Big Bang
comet tails and trails
of stardust

- Beth Buckley

morning star fades clouds drifting from pink to gold

- Paul Walker

first light almost believing an apricot dawn

- Susan King

waking up
before the alarm clock
sunshine in the room

- Hanne Hansen

morning opens
taking a rose
out of its shadow

- Humberto Gatica

pink of dawn the leveret's ears pricked

- Claire Everett

introducing the neighbours scrub-jay

- Beverley Acuff Momoi

first light...
a crab emerges
from the shingle

- Tim Gardiner

high tide —
the skeins of geese link up
to span the sky

- Ian Storr

spawning coral
once a year, the snow
falls upward

- Debbie Strange

returning to the sea
the seal pup's eyes
of obsidian

- Mark Gilbert

from source to sea
the old waterwheel
churning up the day

- Mark Gilfillan

soft fingertips
turn red -
the bite of strings

- Lucy Courtney-Brisbane

throwing wide the curtains
to sickle moon
& woodpigeons

- Colin Blundell

outback highway
crows hopscotch
to fresh roadkill

- Marietta McGregor

inch by inch
the necks of farmyard geese
and the new colt

- Sheila K. Barksdale

sun above the oaks
a dusty Ganesh
squats on a shelf

- Dennis Tomlinson

flickering oil lamps
around the ancient tree
the temple grows

- Madhuri Pillai

long golden hair
billowing in the breeze
carving symbols in stone
(M. Maier, Atalanta fugiens, 1618)

- Tim Stone

Japanology -
in the full moon
now a hare

- Gérard Krebs

dappled light
two ringlet butterflies
courting...

- Caroline Skanne

on the wings
of a butterfly, the orange
I carry home

- Kala Ramesh

a frog jumps in
the way the universe
expands ...

- Robert B. McNeill

a full bucket
lifted out
into daylight

- Gunita Zaube

watching clouds:
a dragon, a horse
then all is gone

- Lesley Prince

deer in my garden
their bones remember
the wolves

- Charles Christian

hyena cub cull
the alpha female's calls
echo against the hill

- Karen Hoy

slender hazel trunk
a single ivy vine
taking a chance

- Geoffrey Winch

Sunday morning
breaking the silence
a lone church bell

- Peter Morriss

a softening
that point where snow
becomes rain

- John Parsons

breathing in and out
almost imperceptible
the rhythm of life

- Diane M. Mayo

child's high chair—
oh the things
you will launch

- Scott Mason

courtyard
a toddler touches the tip
of a camellia bud

- Beverley George

first painting
the toddler proudly shows
a cat with five legs

- Ron Woollard

colouring book
the child magics beggars
into kings

- Nick Sherwood

museum tour
open young faces
with blank sketchbooks

- Ian Turner

Sunday evening
small children coming
down the slides

- Pruthvi Shrikaanth
(Assistant editor, age 10)

clonk clonk clonk
a little girl shuffles past
in her mother's heels

- Phillip Murrell

school's out
the breeze
of children
running past

- Michael Smeer

a pink Pegasus
protruding from the rucksack
departure lounge

- Ralph Stott

uni open day
every young person
tagging along a parent

- Basem Farid

rainy morning
mum's jam brings
a whiff of summer

- Iliyana Stoyanova

elderflower jelly
wobbles me back
to childhood

- Amanda Bell

Angelus bells
children, trees, coots
and my creaky knees

- Norbert Hirschhorn

too late to retreat
the smell of jasmine
by your gate

- Doreen King

fragrant blossoms
we whisper under cones
of moonlight

- Jan Benson

his fishing gear
on e-bay
- the boy's in love

- Andrew Shimield

fresh primulas
on the windowsill
of the deceased

- Ruth Hanchett

squinting to see
two faint lines
counting moons

- Lyndsey Toon

second pregnancy
the smell
of turned earth

- Frances Angela

a bough
heavy with snow–
her baby's first kick

- Claire Knight

springtide—
the swell of her belly
when the baby rolls

- Carole MacRury

safely stowed
in the cot
the coming child

- Robert Smith

unchartered...
the first few steps
of our baby

- Josette Attard

crowded
by the inevitable boxes
where to now?

- Veronica Shimanovskaya

at the gate
our possessions, colour coded
fill the removal van

- Ruth Tyers

removal day –
our pictures' imprints
left behind

- Martin Caley

my new home:
I have traded sunsets
for this sunrise

- Dee Evetts

moving in
no faces in the pictures
that I hang

- Alison Williams

debut lap-tray meal...
a lone sepia print
crowning the tv

- Malcolm Williams

a shout
from one of the tents:
night darkened further

- Hisahi Miyazaki

streets of childhood
all the faces
strangers now

- Rachel Sutcliffe

starting her memoir
not with
a childhood

- Katherine Gallagher

wind swirled
spirals of white ashes
at last - she can fly

- Jim Curry

how to move forward
knowing that she was only
as good as her last song

- Maxine Bracher

in the graveyard –
buds close
to opening

- John Gonzalez

wild gardenia
whitens along the path—
first father-daughter dance

- Mary Jo Balistreri

icy path
his girlfriend's father
refuses to melt

- Kevin Goldstein-Jackson

camp fire
the girl I like
decides to go blonde

- John Kinory

clutching documents
outside the estate agents
rain clouds part

- Caroline Robson

move in together
our two teapots utilised
alternately

- Diane Davy

dropped coffee cup
a nightmare
in the making

- Michael Scott

matching socks
the long sigh
back to work

- David Serjeant

morning train
the waft of someone's
egg sarnies

- John Rowlands

tong tong pop
the aroma of fresh coffee
pours out

- Graham Murray

first past the post:
crowshit
on our window

- Helen Buckingham

walking a local lane
he insists
he knows it well

- Ann Thomas

first row
the soprano's perfect
teeth

- Stella Pierides

window cleaner –
the blue rinse
of tattoos

- Chris Luck

goodbye note
the rhythmic tick
of the kitchen clock

- Bob Lucky

my tweets @dawn
yours @dusk, do the same birds
chorus #downunder

- Marc Evans

journeys
chalked up in the blue
the bathtub overflows

- Jean Curnow

a Kerouac paperback
gives birth to
a Kodachrome slide

- Hamish Ironside

old belongings
the flash of a golden key
changes the direction

- Auriciéia Dumke

recession on New Year's Day—
glasses of cult wine cork-tainted

- Francis Attard

ontological fear
within the heart
the lotus

- Mel Ledgard

a small boy studies the mummy of

- J. Mark Ritchie

just
one unicorn
that's all it takes

- Leo Lavery

one door in a field
the mason opens it
first things first

- Derek Hughes

peasants sing . . .
not knowing all their songs
are dying

- Gabriel Rosenstock

that early goal
still the best
of the season

- Peter Butler

cutting the pack
the bland stare of
the Queen of Spades

- David Cobb

closing ceremony
the world comes together
for a selfie

- Ian Willey

in and out of my dreams
the ancient lift
creaks again

- Maggie West

my first grey hair
yet I am not
an éminence grise

- Ruth E Parker

picking up
friendships left behind
les neiges d'antan

- Dick Pettit

a day to myself...
I follow the river
back to its source

- Thomas Powell

next year's diary
its blank pages
holding secrets

- Catherine Redfern

Index of Poets

Previous BHS Members' Anthologies

1992	Sea	2004	Other
1993	Fire	2005	River
1994	Hill	2006	Light
1995	Sky	2007	Storm
1996	Home	2008	Building
1997	Away	2009	Earth
1998	Island	2010	Celebration
1999	Forest	2011	Gift
2000	Space	2012	Air
2001	Flat	2013	Time
2002	Hidden	2014	Sound
2003	Path	2015	Edge

Printed by:

booksfactory.co.uk